CHRISTPOWER

CHRISTPOWER
JOHN SHELBY SPONG

FROM THE ORIGINAL PROSE BY
JOHN SHELBY SPONG

ARRANGED IN FREE VERSE BY
LUCY NEWTON BOSWELL

ST. JOHANN PRESS

Published in the United States of America
by St. Johann Press
P.O. Box 241
Haworth, NJ 07641

Originally published in 1975: Hale Publishing Company

Library of Congress Cataloging-in-Publication Data

Spong, John Shelby.
   Christpower / John Shelby Spong ; from the original prose by John
Shelby Spong arranged in free verse by Lucy Newton Boswell.—Rev. ed.
      p. cm.
   ISBN 10: 1-878282-11-5 (alk. paper)
   ISBN 13: 978-1-878282-11-8 (alk. paper)
   1. Meditations. 2. Jesus Christ—Meditations. I. Boswell, Lucy
Newton. II. Title.

BV4832.3.S66 2007
232—dc22

                                          2007060738

The paper used in this publication meets the minimum requirements of the American
National Standard for Information Sciences—Permanence of Paper for Printed Library
Materials, ANSI/NISO Z39/48-1992

Manufactured in the United States of America

OTHER BOOKS BY JOHN SHELBY SPONG:

HONEST PRAYER

DIALOGUE: IN SHEARCH OF JEWISH-CHRISTIAN UNDERSTANDING
    (with Jack Daniel Spiro)

LIVING COMMANDMENTS

EASTER MOMENT

INTO THE WHIRLWIND: THE FUTURE OF THE CHURCH

BEYOND MORALISM: A CONTEMPORARY VIEW OF THE TEN
    COMMANDMENTS
    (with Denise Haines)

SURVIVAL AND CONSCIOUSNESS

LIVING IN SIN? A BISHOP RETHINKS HUMAN SEXUALITY

RESCUING THE BIBLE FROM FUNDAMENTALISM

BORN OF A WOMAN

RESURRECTION: MYTH OR REALITY

LIBERATING THE GOSPELS: READING THE BIBLE WITH JEWISH EYES

HERE I STAND: MY STRUGGLE FOR A CHRISTIANITY OF INTEGRITY, LOVE
    AND EQUALITY

A NEW CHRISTIANITY FOR A NEW WORLD

THE SINS OF SCRIPTURE

JESUS FOR THE NON-RELIGIOUS

IN MEMORIAM
WILLIAM CONWELL SPONG 1933-2004
My brother in fact and in faith

PREFACE

It is a rare thing for a book to have a reincarnation more than 30 years after its original date of birth. However, that has been the fate or perhaps the destiny of this volume. It was born of sermons preached in St. Paul's Episcopal Church in downtown Richmond, Virginia, during the years of 1973 and 1974. I was a 42-year-old priest struggling even then with the question of how to communicate a Christianity formed by the gospels of the first century of this Common Era to a generation living in the late 20th century of this Common Era. How can one cling to the substance but not the form of that faith system? Those issues still consume me today but now we have moved into the 21st century. The frightened religious mentality of today's world has become so brittle, so hard and unbending that its adherents resist these efforts with increasing tenacity. The religiously alienated, who would rather have no religion than the one with which they are so regularly confronted, choose not to bother with these issues at all.

On the years between the book's birth and this reprinting, I have published a number of titles like, *Living in Sin? A Bishop Rethinks Human Sexuality*; *Rescuing the Bible from Fundamentalism, Born of a Woman, Resurrection: Myth or Reality, Liberating the Gospels: Reading the Bible with Jewish Eyes, Why Christianity Must Change or Die, Here I Stand: My Struggle for a Christianity of Integrity, Love and Equality, A New Christianity for a New World, The Sins of Scripture* and *Jesus for the Non-Religious*. What became obvious to me as these volumes came off the press was that in book after book, I was addressing the questions I had raised in *Christpower*. This was particularly true about the last book, *Jesus for the Non-Religious* in which I made the connection overt. That is what prompted the reprinting of this treasured volume.

Are there changes in the text? Yes, indeed, but I doubt if the average reader would ever notice. In 1973-74, when these words were first formed, my sensitivity to inclusive language had not yet been born. God was regularly referred to as He, Him or His. Human beings were called mankind and man. I have gone through the texts and changed those words that today seem so offensive. It is amazing how deep the revolution in language has been through which the western world has journeyed in the last 30 years or so. At least, my journey in this arena has been significant.

Poetry evokes images, fires the imagination and opens words to new meanings. It has always been the better way to talk about the God who can be experienced but not known. I am grateful to the one who helped me shape these words so many years ago and even more grateful that they have a chance to be born anew and to live even in the complex realities of the 21st century.

This volume was originally dedicated to my brother, William Connell Spong. Our friendship, which was both deeply personal and obviously professional, was broken by the only power that could ever have broken it on February 3, 2004, when Will died unexpectedly in his sleep. It is now republished "In Memoriam." He was my only brother, the third sibling in our family's list of three. My sister Betty Boyce Spong Marshall and I remain to recall him and give thanks for what he meant to both of us.

John Shelby Spong
Morris Plains, New Jersey
February 27, 2007

PROLOGUE   From the Church at Large:

In a novel of a generation or so ago, there is woven a story of a close personal relationship in which nothing seems to go right for one of the people involved, and disaster appears imminent for the relationship. Somewhere along the line, in an abrasive verbal confrontation, the unhappy character in the story levels with the other and reveals her feelings in these words: "You give me the power to continue my life but not the power to lose it."

If we are insightful and reasonably honest with ourselves, we are able to say the identical thing about some of the dilemmas posed for us in significant daily relationships in which we share. Education is a very important dynamic in our lives, and sometimes we try to coerce it into doing too much: It can give us the power to continue our life but not the power to lose it. Financial security, while much more tenuous, is another important dynamic whose limits we tend to overextend beyond its inherent stress factor. It can also give us the power to continue but not the power to lose our life.

The author of this volume has written (or spoken) CHRISTPOWER out of an abiding conviction that a total commitment by a person to Jesus Christ our Lord, is able to provide the saving dynamic which can lift us off the horns of our dilemma and there enable us to do both: continue our life, but in a much more profound dimension because we have been led to lose our life – for Christ's sake! One of his literary gems states it thusly:

> Would we know this Christ?
>   Then we must open ourselves
>   to all that life means.
>   We must dare to love
>   and dare to live.
>   We must learn
>   to give ourselves away freely –
>   waste love! grasp life! decide to be!
> Be open to the
>   love,
>   acceptance,
>   forgiveness
> that is the meaning of Christ;
> and live in this power,
>   knowing the deepest secret of life.
> In these few lines the entire work is encapsulated.

The Reverend John Shelby Spong, rector of St. Paul's Church, Richmond, Virginia, is one of the new breed of Episcopal priests and parish rectors, whose commitment to exploring both the mystery and the practical transforming alchemy of the Christian faith is infusing vitality into a time-honored, storied, downtown parish church and – not so incidentally – leavening for good the political, religious, and social life of an entire city. He is an engaging preacher and an effective mind-stretching teacher. Nor does he neglect the exercise of his extensive pastoral gifts.

The substance of CHRISTPOWER emanated from the pulpit of St. Paul's Church Sunday after Sunday. Unfortunately, like the poetically-enshrined "desert flower," sermons, which deserve a livelier fate, too often are "born to blush" unheard, wasting "their fragrance on the desert air." Lucy Boswell has chosen to volunteer her considerable talents, transliterating John Spong's sermons into free verse form, in the expectation that they will fare better than the fabled desert flower in the hearts and minds of readers of this unique volume. For one can only conclude that venturesome readers are bound to be enriched by CHRISTPOWER.

A serendipity resulting from this published volume could be a revival of concern about the caliber of preaching in the Church and a timely rededication on the part of many to the art of the preaching of the Word.

Highlands, North Carolina
March 1975

John E. Hines
Presiding Bishop 1964-1974
Protestant Episcopal Church

I believe in Christpower.

Like sunshine and air and salted oceans, Christpower is of the public domain. No laws can rule it, no restrictions can limit it, no thing can contain it. Christpower can never be the private property of any person or group of persons. When spontaneously shared, its nature is to mightily increase.

Christpower is of God, begetting life and life and more life. Not bound by human order or any concept that the mind can conceive. Christpower has neither equal nor substitute, and it only springs forth from the depth of being of all life. Its glorious wonder is the joy of living communion.

Lucy Newton Boswell

PART 1
THE CHRIST

Christ is no longer an object of religion, but something quite different, really the Lord of the world.

The Christian...like Christ himself, must drink the earthly cup to the lees, and only in his doing so is the crucified and risen Lord with him, and he is crucified and risen with Christ.

Christ takes hold of a man (and a woman) at the center of his (or her) life.

Dietrich Bonhoeffer
Letters and Papers from Prison

We are to find God in what we know,
Not in what we do not know.

Dietrich Bonhoeffer
Letters and Papers from Prison

Look at him!

Look not at his divinity,
　　　　but look, rather, at his freedom.
Look not at the exaggerated tales of his power.
　　　　but look, rather, at his infinite capacity to give himself away.
Look not at the first-century mythology that surrounds him,
　　　　but look, rather, at his courage to be,
　　　　　　his ability to live,
　　　　　　　　the contagious quality of his love.

　　　Stop your frantic search!
Be still and *know* that this is God:
　　　　this love,
　　　　　　this freedom,
　　　　　　　this life,
　　　　　　　　this being;

　　　and
when you are accepted,
　　　　accept yourself;
when you are forgiven,
　　　　forgive yourself;
when you are loved,
　　　　love yourself.
　　Grasp that Christpower
　　　　and
　　dare to be yourself!

Not knowing who we are,
    we walk in darkness.

To the ancient ancestors of the human race,
each night brought something of terror and devastation.
         No street lights.
         No candle lights.
         No neon signs.
               Darkness.
A darkness that our primitive forbears could not dispel.
Not surprisingly,
   whatever hurled back the darkness
   became the object of ancient worship:
     the sun, the moon, the stars, and fire.

The worshipped symbols of light versus the demonic powers
Of darkness.

   The Prince of Darkness reigned supreme
   in the distortions of the purpose of God's creation.

When Christians tell about the birth of their Lord,
They speak of a powerful light that
               split the darkness of night:
       "A light to lighten the Gentiles."

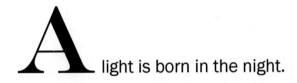
light is born in the night.

Born is a life whose power of love dispels darkness,
banishes demons,
heals sicknesses,
restores life
calls people into a new creation.
His is a life that reveals what all life was created to be:
free, whole, giving, loving.

"In him was life,
and his life was the light of men and women,
and his life shines in darkness,
and the darkness cannot extinguish it."

Love restores life to its true purpose

and
light is revealed when love touches us
and
enables us to grasp our humanity,
fulfill our potential,
live out our destiny.

"I am the light of the world.
The one who follows me
will not walk in darkness
but will have the light of life."

Jesus The Christ

reveals the
Source of Life, the
Ground of Being, the
Power of Love;
and so we worship this Life.
We worship him
by
living in his freedom,
sharing in his being,
giving of his love;
and
we call him
Lord!

Saviour!   **T**he Son of the living God!

God,
The life of Jesus of Nazareth
reveals to me the very nature of all being,
      and because

   to me,

         is the Source of Life,
         the Source of Love,
         the Ground of Being,
   I can see God in Jesus,
         the free, whole human being.

I stand in awe of this life,
      this Christ,
      who is all that life is meant to be.
Jesus of Nazareth is
      Son of God,
            begotten, not made,
                  light of light,
                        very God of very God.

My awe and my reverence for this life can,
            and does,
      easily become worship.

Jesus and Christ:

They are not the same.

Jesus was a person;   Christ is a title,
a theological principle.

Christ is beyond history.

Jesus was of history;

Jesus was human,
            finite,
                limited;   Christ is power divine,
                        infinite,
                            unlimited.

Jesus had a mother and father,
a human heritage.
He was born
        and
            he died.   Christ is beyond
the capacity of the mind
to embrace.

The name of our Lord
is
Jesus of Nazareth
through whom the God of life,
love, and being
is revealed
and thus about whom men and women made the startling and revolutionary claim:
You Are the Christ.

This is what the Bible means by the title *Christ*:
            living,
            eternal,
            God-given power
            breaking into human life.

W hy am I convinced?
    Because I have seen people
        resurrected by love.
    I have watched beauty
        transcend ugliness,
    love
        overcome hatred,
    faith
        transform fear,
    life
        overcome death.

This
        is Christpower,
   and it is not alien or foreign
        to our world.

Would we know this Christ?

Then we must open ourselves
to all that life means.
We must dare to love
and dare to live.
We must learn
to give ourselves away freely –
waste love! Grasp life! Decide to be!

Be open to the

love,
acceptance,
forgiveness
that is the meaning of Christ;
and live in this power,
knowing the deepest secret of life.

To be in Christ

          is
              to come alive.

To be in Christ
       is
to turn on to life,
to discover the fullness of living.

To be in Christ
       is
          to know the power of love,
             to experience freedom,
                wholeness,
                   being.

We
    will reveal the glory of God,
        so abundantly present in Jesus,
when we too are set free
        to be the self we were created to be,
as he was set free
        to be the self he was.

Only in this way do we imitate him.

So immense is the power of

    Christ,
so deep is his appeal
        that
at every stage in life
we seem to see him
      from a different angle,
to see him with new insight.

Our Christ
    is like
the sea beneath the sun;
      ever changing,
      yet ever the same.

I am

the Vine: the sustainer of life.

I am

the Light: the vanquisher of darkness.

I am

the Good Shepherd: the essence of outgoing caring.

I am

the Bread: the food that passes not away.

I am

the Resurrection: the source of all life.

Those of us who believe in this Christ,

though we die,

yet shall we live.

The world was here

before we were born;
it shall be here
after we are no more.
Life does not go on forever,
and we wonder:
If a person dies, shall that person live again?
The Christian story is a story of
One
who seemed infinitely to transcend his barriers,
even the barrier of death:
His ability to be open was uncompromised;
he lived out a freedom and a wholeness;
his capacity for love revealed
that he had received
an infinite amount of love,
a love that continued to flow
even
as his life was being destroyed.
As he died, he lived.

This life, this love, tested that ultimate barrier of death,
and witnesses were convinced that he prevailed,
generating power that other lives have met
in age after age
setting them free to live,
to press the limits of their potential,
to become persons they never dreamed
they could be.

If a person dies, shall that person live again?
Does that which is my most true self
    transcend the reality of death?

Love transcends death,
              and if love does,
so also does life;
    for
        life –
           real life –
is always the child of love.

              If love has entered a person's life,
touched that person's being,
      lifted that person beyond all limits,
         given that person a glimpse of life's deepest meaning,
         nothing
         can separate that person from its transforming power;
         and
    life lived in this power
         does live again and will live again.

Death

will be only a barrier that
    can be pressed and
        overcome.

The reality I call God
is beyond the power of the human mind
     fully to grasp,
beyond the ability of human words
     finally to capture,
beyond the feeble attempts of human beings
     ever completely to describe.

We grope after the truth, and
we see only through a glass darkly.

nd who is God?

He is not a being in the sky
who thinks and acts,
who feels and directs.
od
is
the Source of life;
so God is seen wherever life is lived,
and God is not alien or separate from
that life.

God
is
the Source of love;
so God is seen wherever love is shared,
and God is not alien or separate from
that love.

God
is
the Ground of being;
so God is seen wherever one has the courage to be,
and God is not alien or separate from
that being.

In,
with,
under
every human meeting,
    there is an eternal
Thou,
    holy God.

When we touch this holy power,

eternal Thou,
we experience the purpose of creation
and
we know the meaning of life.

In Jesus of Nazareth

the fullness of life is lived,
the depth of love is shared,
the courage to be all that one is, is revealed.
So Jesus reveals
life
and love
and being.
Jesus reveals

God,

and whenever God is seen
in human life,
we call that power *Christ*.

Look closely at Jesus of Nazareth.

There you will see a human being at rest,
    being what he was meant to be,
        freeing those around him to be themselves,
            calling them by the power of love
            into a new acceptance of their humanity.

    Look at the peace that marked his life.
Look at his ability to cross any frontier
    and embrace any reality.
        Secure.
            Affirmed.
                Whole.

Touch his power and know
                what Christians have meant through the ages:
        Saviour!
            Lord!
                Christ!

I am the Bread of life."

The author of the Fourth Gospel
    wrote about the turn of the first century,
    rather late in Christian history.
The writer does not pretend to present
    the Jesus of history, but rather,
    the Christ of meditation;
        not literal words,
            but profound truths
       that only one who knew the Christ
       could ever articulate.
The Fourth Gospel is a meditation
          on the power of Christ
          and the meaning of life.
This is the author who has his Christ say:
       "I am the Bread of life."

John records no account of the Last Supper.

Never in this narrative does Jesus take bread,
          bless it,
            break it,
              give it.
Because when the Christ is nailed to the cross,
        this is the moment for this author in which
          The Bread of Life
      is broke and given.
There we see that power that feeds life
       so that it never hungers again.
There love is revealed,
    and we see who he is in the magnificent picture
      of the free person
        giving life to all the world.

Jesus said to them:
  "I am the bread of life.
  The one who comes to me will not hunger."
Bread – food, eating: a symbol for love.
    As bread physically fills the body,
        so love psychologically fills a life.
Christ claims the power that
      fulfills the deepest needs of human life,
      which do not change from age to age.
          "I am the bread of life."
All life is lonely, insecure.
All life hungers and thirsts for wholeness, for being.
All life seeks that elusive something that satisfies.
            But we never find it.
Life hungers for the food that passes not away.
    We know that
        love is the power that sets us free to be;
        love is that which gives us our humanity;
        love is required in order to achieve life and wholeness;
    so wherever in life we find love in an ultimate sense,
        we will find our Saviour.
If that love is present in Jesus of Nazareth,
        he has a claim to the title *The Christ of God*.
If this Jesus can satisfy the insatiable yearnings of our humanity,
        then we too can call him Lord,
    and we will see him in every experience of life that
        feeds,
            fulfills,
                sustains.
We call him
        Lord!
            Saviour!
              Christ!
    who is the bread of life.

Jesus Christ: a person with a destiny;

yet in the grip of this destiny he is free,
    for it is a destiny he chooses,
        a destiny in which he is fulfilled,
           a destiny through which he gives of himself
           to the world.
But he discovers that
    freedom is not free,
    and the inevitable price of his freedom
        is loneliness,
        dreadful loneliness,
    the loneliness of one who knows where he is going
        but
is surrounded by those who cannot accept or understand.

Loneliness.
        "You are the Christ of God."
        "Peter, this is my unique Son. Why don't you hear him?"
        "Hosannah!"

        "Could you not watch with me one brief hour?"

The loneliness of being who you are in a world
        that does not understand.
Yet
    this free man is not at the mercy of his loneliness.
        Jesus does not
            grasp at the fulfillment of approval,
               compromise his integrity,
                   need to be affirmed by anyone,
I   for Jesus is at one with himself,
    bearing the existential power of the radically free man.

    am not alone, because the Holy One is with me."

It was an unusual parade!

The crowd was happy; the mood was light.
    Hosannah!
Festivity, palm branches, excitement, adulation.
They called him "king."
They would make him their ruler.

       But on he rode.

What a difference a week can make!
    The crowds have dwindled from a happy throng
       to

a scared few:
One twelve,
      eleven,
        three.
ne lonely man.
       But on he rode.

Here is a whole person,

free to be what he is even as the crowds shout
"Hosannah!"
free to be what he is even as the crowds shout
"Crucify!"

In this life we see God.

To be touched by this life is
to share in his power,
to taste his freedom,
to possess his peace.
To be touched by this life is
to know ourselves to be
loved,
affirmed,
set free
to live in the glorious liberty of the children of God.

"For if the Son shall set you free, then you are free indeed."

Jesus was a possessed person,

possessed by an all-consuming purpose:
        to reveal the life-giving power of love,
a revelation that had to come at the exact time
and under the exact circumstances,
        or it would not be grasped.
It was to be the grand finale of
            this life,
and it had to be acted out in
            Jerusalem.
Jerusalem drew Jesus inevitably.
"For this came I forth."
        "My time has not yet come."

When the moment does arrive,
        Jesus sets his face steadfastly toward that city
        which holds the key to his destiny,
        drawing him like a magnet.
He does not waver or deviate.
Finally,
        in the Garden of Gethsemane Jesus proclaims:
            "The time is at hand for all things to be accomplished."

A possessed man, a man with a destiny.
        His dying words are the cry:
            "It is finished!"

No episode in the life of Jesus

more deeply revealed who Jesus the Christ was
than did
the crucifixion.

So affirmed was his life
by the love of his God
that his security,
                his presence,
                        his very being
could not be destroyed by
death;
and in this being
he could reach out in love
even to those who
                would take his life
                away.
Because the ground of his being
was beyond the power of
death,
        Jesus
was able willingly to allow his life to be
destroyed.

Even at the moment of death
the life of Jesus expressed the love of God,
                        the caring of God,
                        the infinite giving of God.

    In awed silence
the soldiers who had tortured him watched,
and when his life was ended, it was a soldier
who said, "Truly
this man was the Son of God!"

group of the disciples came together

after the trauma of the cross.
They discussed the relationship they had had with
    Jesus of Nazareth.
They tried to fit together the broken pieces of
    their life with him.
His death was incomprehensible, seeming to be
    a total negation of the meaning of his life.
In their minds, his death called into question
    his love, his freedom, his power.
They saw his death as God's "no" to all of the hopes
    they had centered in him.

But still that death made no sense, for
    the beauty they had known was real.
The security, the capacity to give, the ability to love;
    God could not say "no" to that
    and still be God.

Their minds remained a cauldron of confusion.

While they talked, the time came for the evening meal,
    and as they ate
they remembered!

The last meal they had eaten together...
on the night of the betrayal...
such a strange meal...
remember...

Broken bread, *this is my body;*
poured out wine, *this is my blood.*
When you gather together, do this
in memory of me, for whenever
you eat this bread and
drink this cup, you
             "show forth the Lord's death until he comes."
Remembering,
reenacting,
suddenly
they saw!
      Death did not negate Jesus of Nazareth.
Rather, it revealed the fullness of his love,
his freedom to give himself away,
his capacity to absorb the
        hate-filled,
           hurtful distortions
              of human life.
           Death did not destroy Jesus of Nazareth.
Rather, it revealed his inner meaning,
his secret power.

When they understood this,
      they saw Jesus victorious over death.
They saw love and life and freedom,
      and they, renewed, resurrected,
dared to step forward boldly to claim
      that power for themselves.

This
was Easter.

This is what lies behind John's story of the risen Lord
by the Sea of Galilee,
talking to Every person, Every person whose name is Peter:

"Peter, do you love me?
Peter, can you feel my love for you so deeply
that you can trust that love?
It is a love that knows your failure, Peter,
          your weakness,
               your fear,
                    your insecurity,
                         your façade,
     even your act of denial.
It is you I love, Peter. Can you believe that
     so you can respond in answering love?"

"Yes, Lord," Peter answers.
"In my own halting, inadequate, scared way,
I love you."
"Well, Peter, Everyman," says that risen Christ.
"If you love me, share that love
     with one another.
Feed my sheep.
Be sensitive to those like yourself all around you.
Love them into shedding their masks;
     love them into living.
Give them hope, understanding.
For it is for this purpose, Peter,
     that I have lived,
                    died,
                         and risen again –
that all might have life, real life,
and that they might have it
          abundantly."

C "He is not here," they said.
"He has been raised."

hristpower.

As it was in the beginning,
it is now,

A nd so shall it ever be.

PART 2
THE CHURCH

It is through what he (she) himself (herself) is, plus what he (she) receives, that a person becomes a complete entity.

...human relationships are the most important thing in life...God uses us in God's dealings with others.

The Church is the Church only when it exists for others.

Dietrich Bonhoeffer
Letters and Papers from Prison

Church
has nothing to do with denominations
buildings
institutions.
It has everything to do with shared life
shared love
the communion of saints
the forgiveness of sins.
Church has nothing to do with authority
valid orders
a privileged priesthood.
It has everything to do with caring
ministering
loving
being.
Church is any community in which there is Christpower
present.

The Christian faith says:

Be yourself, yes,
>   but
>   judge the self you are
>   by
>   the standard of what you can become.

We Christians are ordinary men and women
who happen to possess an extraordinary mission.
        We are typical specimens of humanity.
We can be petty and argumentative,
                hostile,
                    bitter,
                        spiteful,
                            selfish.
        We can be hurtful and even mean;
        but
we can also be magnanimous and real,
        open and loving,
            generous and humble.
    We can be warm and forgiving
        and,
                wondrous though it seems,
                time after time,
                person after person in
                generation after generation
        finds
            life,
                love,
                    wholeness
        in our midst.
We exist that all people might know of God's love for them.

The greatest thing that we, your Church, can do for you,
    Marianne,
is to help you develop your capacity to love,
    for this we believe is the secret of life
      both here and hereafter.
If you have the capacity to love,
        to give,
        to invest yourself in others,
     then you can know
       what it means to be alive,
       what it means to be human,
       what it means to be *you*.
Our task as the Church is
  to share God's love with you
until your capacity to love is so developed
    that you are able to love yourself
    and
    to make this love available to all others.
It is our hope that in this vital task,
      our Church mission,
       we shall not fail you or our God.

Our names are
Susanna and Fitzhugh.

As very young infants,
our first and most elemental need is for
            your love.
We are not born with the capacity to love
            either ourselves or others.
                        To us
the world seems very strange and hostile,
even cold and distant.
                  We do not bring
into our lives a sense of our own value
                        or worth
                        or dignity –
that has to be given to us.
                  You will teach us
to value ourselves
            only as you value us.
                  We will
love and accept ourselves
            only as you love and accept us.

We cannot give love
until we have received it.
We cannot escape our self concerns
until we are secure in your acceptance.
So
give us your love and your lives,
introduce us through your love and caring
to the God of love,
and
long before we can ever say God's name,
help us to experience God's power.
Care for us until we can care for others.

Give us your smile,
your hand,
your touch,
your embrace.

Be sensitive to us even

when we are small and helpless.

Let us experience Church as
a warm feeling,
a place where love is lived,
a place where we belong.
Do not make us aliens in the house of God.

So take us in
and let us share
with you.

Teach us, Susanna and Fitzhugh,
    what it means to be part of a living history.
Hand on to us the faith of the ages.

Prepare us to be adults who will stand
    in the faith of our fathers and mothers.
Prepare us to be receivers
    of the truth of the past
and dwellers
    in the truth of the present,
so that we can be dispensers
    of the truth to the future.

Let our lives be planted and rooted
    in the soil of a living heritage
        which we must receive
    from you.

Between our entry into this family at baptism
and
that distant moment when we depart
this life at death,
        we will live through many stages,
                many crises,
                many experiences.

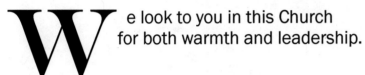e look to you in this Church
for both warmth and leadership.

There will be times when
life will be confused
and choices clouded,
and we will want to hear from you
the words of
authority and power and discipline.
We want you
to know who you are, what you believe,
and what your faith demands of you
in terms of ethical action.
We want you
to have the courage of your convictions,
to act upon your faith,
to be willing to lead
with strength
and to speak
with decisiveness.
We want to look to you
for moral power and leadership,
for standards of conduct.
Does not your faith require that?

There will be other times when
        we will need and want a
        soothing, caring, sustaining strength.
You know our hearts will be broken many times
        during our lives. We will know
        pain and bereavement.
We will be hurt,
        and someone will have to lift us up,
        mend our wounds, and
        give us the courage to face life again.

Even when we become adults
        life will sometimes knock us down.
We want you to let us be dependent children
        when we are hurting.
We want you to care for us
        when we fall.
                Give us the freedom to fail,
                the courage to rise again from the ground and walk.
Be the rock of love under our feet,
                the everlasting arms always beneath us.

We ask you to be sensitive
        to the world in which we will live.
It will not be your world.
        It is not today's world or yesterday's world.
            Our world
            is tomorrow's world.
We look to you to prepare us
        to live in tomorrow.

        Do not blind our spirits
with the prejudices of yesterday.
        Do not poison our hearts
with the hatreds and fears of your generation.

        Let us be free to find God
        in the accents of our generation.
We want, and our lives will require,
        a Church family of broad perspective and wide variety,
        for
        we want and need
                a gospel we can believe,
                a Christ we can serve,
                a God we can worship
        in the twenty-first century.

We,
        Susanna and Fitzhugh,
look to you for these foundation stones of life.

Our human search for the community
                that overcomes our loneliness
is finally nothing less than a search for
                the Holy Spirit.

Holy Spirit enhances life,
                opens life,
                        expands life.

Holy Spirit frees us to abandon ego-building exclusiveness,
        allows us to break down the barriers which protect and divide,
                enables us to lay to rest our crippling fears,
                our distorting prejudices.

Holy Spirit makes whole the lives of those it touches.
Holy Spirit calls us into community where
                love is shared,
                        life is real.
Holy Spirit re-creates us in the image of God,
                and
no one can make sense out of God
                until
He or she has glimpsed this Spirit,
                shared this power,
                        known this quality of life.

When I search for the real in life,
inevitably I am led to people experiences.

It is when love is shared with another,
                              openly, deeply, honestly,
that I find true meaning.

It is the understanding concern
        of another
that penetrates the wall of my loneliness
        and allows me to endure.

It is the gift of caring
        that lifts me out of myself
and enables me to give
        in return.

When I experience these things –
                love,
                understanding,
                caring –
I find myself called beyond my limits;
    I discover the courage to be;
        I become something new;
            my life expands.

In direct proportion to the gifts of love
that I have received,
I can walk into new experiences,
break formerly binding barriers,
and be open to those to whom
previously I had been closed.

I find a new reality,
a new joy,
in being the self I am,
for life in touch with love
is a series of
self-transcending experiences.

Trinity
          is
     the fullness of God.

          Trinity
               is
          an invitation to life:
     Join the community! Come as you are!
     Come with
               your doubts,
                    your fears,
                         your faults,
                              your prejudices,
                                   your hang-ups.

Risk being yourself!
Belong!
Know the life-giving power
                         of
                    acceptance and love!
Live in the reality of grace
                              and
open your eyes to the God who stands
                                   over,
                                        under,
                                             around,
                                                  and through our life –
a God whose name is love.

Endlessly
we define

God's love,
God's grace,
God's power,
God's being.

But these are,
and will continue to be,
empty,
dry,
pious clichés
        unless somewhere
        we find
    a community, a life,
    to which
        we can belong
    and in which
        we can give and share our deepest selves
        and build
            a fellowship
                bound by a spirit that is holy,
that enhances life,
frees life,
makes life full and whole.

To the Christian
Sunday was and is the day of resurrection.
The resurrection transformed all life.
The resurrection divided history
into all of that time before Christ
and
all of the rest of the ages that Christ
claims for himself,
Anno Domini,
the years of our Lord.
God's time, God's Sabbath,
is thus not just one day of the week,
but, rather,
in Christ God has claimed *all days*
for God's glory and purpose.
We Christians
make life holy by living as people
aware of the Source of Life,
make love real by loving as people
in touch with the Source of Love.
We participate in resurrection by re-creating life
through our caring,
giving,
sharing.
To claim all life for our Christ
is to keep holy the Sabbath –
a Sabbath that embraces
all time,
all days,
all ages,
all history.
Remember, then,
Keep holy the Sabbath of God!

You shall worship God
    with your mind,
    with your strength,
    with your heart:
a mind
    to search,
        to prove,
            to question,
                to challenge
    that gospel in total honesty;
a strength
    to live out that gospel in the
    difficult and tension-filled arenas
    of injustice and inhumanity;
a heart that is
    open to love,
        on fire with power,
            attuned to the living God.

I need a church that will encourage me
to think,
to probe,
to doubt,
to wrestle,
to search for the truth of God,
        come whence it may, cost what it will.

I believe that the Christian faith is truth,
        but not simplistic truth;
rather, it is truth that searches the deep recesses
of life,
        of human experience,
shedding there its own powerful light.

A Christianity that does violence to the mental processes
        of the modern mind
    will not survive.
A mark of a living Church, I believe,
    is
the freedom to worship God with our Minds.

I need a Church that will call me to Christ,
a Church that will
        challenge my emptiness, my activism,
a Church that will
        hold the Christ before me day and night,
        keeping me
                open,
                    alive,
                        attuned to that presence.

Worship God with all your Heart,
            the center of the life-giving emotions,
            the locus of commitment, conversion,
            which baptizes our minds,
        and
            gives meaning to the activities of our strength.
For a Church to be a living force,
            there must come a moment when we,
                through that Church,
            open our hearts and our lives and say
                "yes!"
            to all of the meaning of Jesus Christ
            and experience his power that turns us on
                to life,
                    to love,
                        to God.

Our priorities must reflect
that this Christ
is the Lord of our lives.
There must be
the glow of praise,
the joy of prayer,
the sense of peace.

I need a Church that will
call me to adore,
dare me to pray,
demonstrate to me the healing power
present in my Lord.
I need a Church that will
show me a living Saviour
and
make appropriate demands on me for response.

This alone fulfills our life.

A Church for me must be daring and courageous.
It must stand on the firing life of life's tensions and controversies,
It must lead its world to new attitudes,
       not simply reflect the old ones;
   It must call, not follow.

To worship God with our Strength is
       to struggle for goodness, for justice,
       to battle oppression,
       to stand to bear witness in the centers of power,
       to call our world to the nobility
           that human life possesses.

This Church,
   if faithful to our Lord,
       will never be a safe haven from tension,
       will never be secure,
       will never be withdrawn,
       will never be uncaring,
       will never be at superficial peace.
We will always be found
       in the troubled waters of life and change.
We will worship God with our strength:
           the strength of our involvement.

I

do not really care about the formula or the words used
to express our faith.
     Words and formulas are not sacred to me.
     They are the earthen vessels through which
        we try to express eternal truth.
     Formulas and words change from age to age.

What I do care about
     is that any words we use to describe
        the God we worship
    must be able also to interpret
        the life we live.
Any statement we make about God
    must
        also be a statement about human beings,
      about life,
        about attitudes,
          about values.
   Otherwise,
theology is but an empty sound, a pious waste of time.

Ibelieve in God the Father-Mother-Creator.
I believe that God is
    the Source of all that is
        and
    that the world is an expression of
        God's life,
            God's joy,
                God's beauty,
                    God's goodness.
Because I believe this,
I must love this world.
    I will
        enter its life,
            participate in its joy,
                experience its beauty,
                affirm its power.

Because I believe in the Father-Mother-Creator,
I have to live so as to enhance the worlds' goodness:
    I will weep over its distortions,
        the violations of its purpose;
    I will yearn to see the world become
        that which it was created to be.

I cannot hate the world,
    refrain from living,
        fear involvement,
    and still say with my lips that
        I believe in God the Father-Mother, the almighty creator.

I believe in God the Son-Redeemer.
I believe that in Jesus of Nazareth
the nature of the creator-God was seen as
    love,
        acceptance,
            forgiveness,
                the fullness of life;
      and
since life is the gift of God,
in him was the fullness of God,
    the self-giving ground of being.

In Jesus of Nazareth I find
    the power that heals my brokenness,
    the forgiveness that redeems my unloveliness.
To believe in Christ, to me,
is to know that I am loved for what I am.
It is to discover the courage
    to be myself,
        to accept my worth, my value, my dignity.
To believe in Christ, to me,
is to live as if the ultimate source of Life,
    the final judge of human beings,
has proclaimed me to be of infinite value.
    Therefore,
I cannot hate myself,
    refuse to be myself,
        or pretend to be someone else.
    I believe in God the Son-Redeemer.

I believe in God the Holy Spirit,
     giver of life,
          sanctifier.
I believe that my redeemed self has
     something to give to others,
that the love that I have known
     must be shared,
that relationships must be formed
     and
community established in which all of us
     are secure enough to risk our lives
          in honesty,
               in forgiveness,
                    in revelation.

Life-giving spirit is that power that
     lifts me out of my loneliness,
          calms my insecurities and fears,
               calls me to share life with another.
God's spirit gives me the courage to be myself
     in honest dialogue with another.
It is God's spirit that enhances my being
     in relation to others.
It is the moments of shared love that
     sanctify human existence and quicken life.
To have these moments
     is to know the meaning of God as Holy Spirit,
          the Lord and Giver of Life.

PART 3
HUMANKIND

To renounce a full life and its real
joys in order to avoid pain is
neither Christian nor human.

I believe that nothing that happens
to me is meaningless....As I see it,
I am here for some purpose, and I
only hope I may fulfill it.

The children of the earth are
rightly proud of being allowed to
shape their own destinies.

Dietrich Bonhoeffer
Letters and Papers from Prison

I come to share life
        and thus
    to bear witness to the Source of Life.

I come to make love real
        and thus
    to bear witness to the Source of Love.

I come to be who I am
        and thus
    to bear witness to the Ground of Being.

The task of the Christian pilgrimage
is to find a way to oneself,
    to discover one's own destiny.

God and our truest self are never found separately,
    but always together.
If we think that we know God
    but do not know ourselves,
        we may be sure that the god we have found
        is an idol.
But if we think we know ourselves
    and do not recognize God as the
    Source of Life,
        we are surely deluded.

The Christian life, in the deepest sense,
    is a seeking and a searching after our own being.

The power of the Christ lay in the fact
    that he lived out his true being:
        He was what he was created to be.
Nothing less than this –
    to be all that *we* were meant to be –
            is our calling in the Christian life.

Yet let us be warned!
In the Christian pilgrimage there is never a point of arrival.
We will never
    achieve the goal of the fulfilled life.
We will never
    be able to rest and exclaim:
        "This is it!"
We will always be
    wanderers,
        discontented people,
        hungering and thirsting after our destiny.

From time to time we will meet another person –
        deeply, genuinely –
or have a transcendent experience.
    In those moments the whole world will seem like home,
        but only for a time;
    and then the search begins anew.

If we accept anything as the ultimate fulfillment,
    the final meaning of life,
and discontinue our search,
    at that moment we, in fact,
        begin to die.

The early Hebrews knew that
sin
is a description of our being
                              not of our doing,
so they spoke of being "born in sin,"
      being "conceived in sin,"
            and passing sin from generation to generation.

Sin, biblically, is the power of inadequate love
      reflected in our inability to live fully.
It is our lack of freedom, our still emerging humanity
      our emotional bondage
      that distorts and twists us,
      making us
            incapable
      of being our deepest selves:
                        whole persons
                        who reflect the image of God.

This is the "sin of the world" that must be
      broken or overcome.
And so we wait,
      and while we wait,
our potential withers until we are
      lifted out of our brokenness.

      We look beyond ourselves
for the external power of love
that can touch and ignite the being of our humanity,
      transforming,
                  fulfilling,
                        freeing
the human nature from which all deeds flow.

We beg the reader of the gospel
not to translate *sin*
                    "evil deed,"
so that *forgiveness* means
                            "divine pardon."

            Rather,
sin must be understood as the manifestation of
            an incomplete humanity
            an evolving self
                    that manifests itself as a
broken, distorted, inadequately loved life,
        for then
forgiveness has a totally different meaning.

    The power that overcomes sin, or that forgives sin,
is the power of love
that goes beneath the deed level of our behavior
and embraces, accepts, and affirms our being,
calling us into
the fullness of life.

        The one who has experienced
this gift of love
manifests it by
                forgiving himself or herself
                        accepting himself or herself
                                loving himself or herself
and being himself or herself
without boasting or apology.

The deepest need of every person
is
to have an authoritative, affirmative
"yes!"
pronounced on his or her life.
When we hear "yes!" said to ourselves,
then we can say "yes!" to others.

Self-acceptance for human beings
is a daily struggle,
while
self-rejection
is easy.
We struggle,
we compete;
we are graded,
judged,
compared.

Our self-doubt is constantly fed.

Jesus Christ is God's "yes!" to men and women,
    not upon our doing,
        but upon our being.
He was affirmed,
    so he could affirm.
    In him,
God is saying, "My nature is love
    and because it is
        my gift is life."
Jesus is God sharing his love with humankind.

When God's "yes!" is heard
        believed,
          responded to,
the life so affirmed is marked by
    a love that is not jealous or selfish,
    a love that keeps no records of wrongs,
    a love that bears all things, endures all things,
    and
a love that shares its own power throughout the world.

Goodness, duty, and moral uprightness
are not the goals of Christianity in the biblical story.
There is morality, but not moralism,
in Christianity.
There is rejection of behavior,
but not rejection of persons.
The judgment found in Christianity
is never separated from love.

The Christ who judges is also the Christ who saves.
Persons are revealed for what they are
only by a love
that accepts them as they are.

Christian judgment is the ability to look at what we are –
our weaknesses,
our sin,
our distortions,
our mutual hurts,
and to see that through it all we have
value,
worth,
dignity;
we are loved!

God judges our deeds
only
because God loves our being.

Stand tall,
be courageous,
fear not even the day of judgment.

One of the unbroken laws of human relationships
          is
that one can never lead or change
those whom one does not love.

        One can never speak
the words of guilt-producing judgment
to those with whom one has not identified
                and still expect to be heard.

        Criticism and judgment
that fall on those for whom one does not deeply care
                is finally intolerable.

        When either righteousness or justice
is separated from deep love and caring,
it is inevitably hostile, and
                it will be repelled.

"Speak the truth," said St. Paul,
"but speak it with love."

I believe that there is a crisis of spirit
                of staggering proportions
        abroad in this land –
        a crisis that could well determine our history
                for the next century,
        a crisis that will not be solved
                until
        we again trust the future and
            have both the faith and the courage to enter it.

I will be accused of giving a simple religious answer
                to our dilemma
        by suggesting that a living God of history,
            who has the whole world in The divine hands,
        is the desperately important missing factor
            in the present moment of time.

I see no other answer.

If God lives,
only then can the future be resurrected
and again achieve reality –
Bomb or no bomb! Terror or no terror!

If the future has hope,
then the present will have meaning
and
the past can be valued.
God is the matrix of our sanity,
the symbol of our hope,
the source of our meaning.

What do we believe about God?
What are we willing to do about it?

No other decision we make,
I believe,
will have quite the same impact
on the history of the world.

There is nothing
that tomorrow can bring
that the God of the Christian faith
cannot transform and redeem.

There is no destruction,
no death so total,
that the living God cannot work through it
to bring life.

In the power of love
bear one another's burden:
          this is the call of our faith.
But if we do not heed that call,
     then the day will come when
          in pain,
               in chaos,
                    in disaster,
          with great ill will,
we shall still have to bear one another's burden.

There is no escape in our tiny, interdependent world.

The choice is a simple one:
     Act now in sensitive love and goodwill,
     or
     fail to act until in anger or tragedy or destruction
     we are engulfed by the problems we
     would not before see.

The choice is ours.

A wilderness in the land of Midian.
A burning bush.
A heavenly voice:
      "Moses, take off your shoes.
      The ground on which you stand is holy ground."

Penetrate the meaning,
      comprehend the power of
this moment in the life of this learned and cultured man,
exiled to the anonymity of the shepherd's role,
      tending his flock on a vast expanse of space.

Because Moses knew that he stood on holy ground,
a new direction for his life began to unfold.

Yet the God of the Bible is never locked into a place,
never limited to a location.
      "You stand now near a burning bush,
      but you will stand
            in the court of Pharaoh,
            in the midst of the Red Sea,
            in the heights of Mt. Sinai,
            in the wilderness looking across the Jordan
                  to the Promised Land.

      The place where you stand is holy ground,
      for God is there."

Have the eyes to see!
    the ears to hear!
        the sensitivity to experience!
Grasp and understand the meaning
    of every present experience,
for the place where you stand in this moment –
    in every moment –
as it was for Moses,
    is holy ground;
for God is seen in
    every gift of love,
        every shared forgiveness,
           every act of caring,
              every moment of beauty.

We too are refugees
    living in an alien lands,
like Moses
    searching for meaning,
        wandering through a dry wilderness of the soul,
          wondering if God still speaks.

"Take off your shoes, Moses,
even in this barren wilderness,
for the ground *wherever* you stand is holy."
So speaks the God who was in the beginning,
                is now,
                and ever shall be.

All of us who are parents
make the perennial mistake:
With the best of intentions,
we seek to impose upon our children
        our solutions,
        our values,
        our standards,
        our methods.

They will not fit.

How hard it is for us to realize
that our young people
do not need our solutions!

        They need
our witness, our example,
                        our encouragement, our freedom;
however,
        they must forge their own solutions,
        create their own values, devise their own methods.

        The most successful parent is the one
        who can give his or her self openly and honestly
        to the child,
        so that the child might find and be
        what he or she most deeply is.

Discontent,
perpetual dissatisfaction,
the presence and knowledge of guilt:
These are the realities of human life, for
to be human
is to envision life more deeply
than any one of us can live it.
To be human
is to see life's potentiality
and against that goal
to look at what one is.
To be human
is to dream the impossible dream of a just society at peace
and then to compare the real world with that dream.
To be human
is never to be content,
never to be satisfied,
never to be at peace.
"In this world you shall have tribulation."
I see in the biblical story no promise of peace of mind,
but
only a peace which passes human understanding:
a peace that can endure the human conflict.
If you have anything in your life
that robs you of being discontented,
that robs you of being dissatisfied,
that provides peace where no peace should be,
then
you may be sure you have become an Idolater;
and
something less than God has your ultimate loyalty,
You have dropped out of life
by dropping out of your humanity.

What, then, does Christianity offer to the discontent
of our human life?
Just this:

The Christian life is the life so fulfilled
by the love of God
that one can live creatively
in the midst of human discontent
without sinking into despair,
that one can face life as it is,
broken and lacking in fulfillment,
and not be depressed.

Being Christian means
that this world can never be so terrible
that we will cease our involvement and commitment
to bring perfection,
though we know
that perfection will never be.
We will not be reduced to inertia.

"Blessed are those who hunger;
blessed are those who thirst."

The Lord is saying:
"Blessed are the discontented,
for they know that they are human.
Blessed are the dissatisfied,
for they refuse to accept what is
for that which can become.
Blessed are those who have not peace of mind
but who live joyfully, gloriously –
without despair, defeat, or inertia,
for they know that the peace of God
does not create contentment,
but instead
enables life to be lived creatively
in the midst of discontentment."

Rejoice in your discontent!
Have the courage to be what you are!
Enter into life and live it!
Celebrate your humanity!
You will discover
that the Lord of life is real,
and that divine power is adequate for all of the pain
of human existence.

Sometimes
I perceive a sense of humor in the Divine
that enables God to laugh
at the wisdom of the world;
at our human pomp and circumstance;
at our values, arrogance, status symbols;
at the infinite lengths we will travel
to broadcast our worth,
    reveal our station in life,
       protect our image,
for this is the way humanity behaves;
while the holy God –
       source of our life,
       ground of our being –
is seen in the gift of love,
lying in a manger
in poverty
in the grimy, insignificant village of Bethlehem.

The discontent of human life proclaims
    that we dream,
        that we envision a self bigger than we are,
        a world larger than we experience.
This dream, this vision
    of what we were meant to be,
    both
    judges us
        and calls us.
    It judges us
    by keeping us dissatisfied.
    It calls us
    by holding the image of fulfillment before us.
In responding to the call of our vision
    we find our human destiny to be ourselves;
        but it is a contradictory destiny,
for our destiny is to accept what we are
    while still being open to become what we can be.

Our humanity requires
    that we have the grace to love what we are
    while
    having the courage to dare
    to grow,
        to change,
            to become a new being at any given moment.

Human beings are creatures with limits,
bounded by a standard and expectation of behavior.
Human beings are not gods.
We are finite.
Our kingdoms do not endure.
We die.
Life is not eternal.
Yet to be human is to possess the freedom
to control our own destiny,
exert responsibility,
know self-transcendence.

All of us have a vision,
a dream,
of the person we want to be –
which is never the same
as what we are.
There, in the gulf between the poles of our humanity,
is the source of our
discontent,
frustration,
quest for power, status, and recognition;
and
this is the level of human restlessness.

Here we experience the absence of peace.

It is this inner struggle to become what we are not yet
that feeds the tensions of life.
It is this inner struggle to become what we are not yet
that announces our humanity.
If we should cease to be discontented,
we also would cease to be human.

Our deepest desire is not found
in earthly symbols of power
or success.
      It is not found in the great
moments of our history
      and certainly not
in the status we seek to acquire.

Our deepest desire is found only in
love –
      powerful, affirming, life-giving love –
that love which always and only comes
      as a gift.

This love is seen
in common things: meeting,
                        sharing,
                        listening
                        loving,
                        being.

This love is the secret
of the Christ.
This love is the
essence of God.

C ome unto me. I will give you rest."

Rest is the quality of being
    that enables us to accept ourselves
    in every stage of life:
        the child's joy and contentment to be a child,
        the adult's willingness to live
            and to accept the responsibilities of adulthood,
        the beautiful dignity of aging with grace.
The rest promised by Jesus of Nazareth
            is rest from the struggle to become
            what we are not;
                it is
                the ability to be what we are.

"Come unto me and I will give you rest."

My peace I give to you,
but not as the world gives."

Peace is that inner security,
    that self-knowledge,
        which enables us to cross any frontier.
            It is
        the capacity to live in any world,
        to respond to any dream.

The world's peace is found in
            status,
                recognition,
                    power –
        which ultimately make us slaves of the system,
        exhausting our energies in a never-ending struggle.

Biblical peace is an inner security
that enables us to
        live in the tensions of life
        without
        being puffed up by success or destroyed by failure.
To possess biblical peace is to have the ability
to walk unafraid
        into any new tomorrow,
        into any new insight,
            and to live in any brave, new world.

"My peace I give to you, but not as the world gives."

Behind every leader in every historic moment
there are hosts of people who produce that leader,
          who support that leader,
              who acknowledge that leader,
                  whose actions make that leadership possible.
          No one leads unless people will follow.
But leadership takes many forms.
Sometimes leaders are found in the army of foot soldiers
who will do the little things,
          the simple things,
              the supportive things,
                  the loving things
          that in concert will create a new environment.

What can we do?

Can we not speak the word of reason and hope
in the midst of emotion and anguish?
          Every contribution, every little gift –
              five loaves and two fishes –
          will help.
          Every calm word will bring peace
          to the troubled waters.

We can open doors to understanding and reconciliation.
We can create an environment of love,
                        concern,
                        goodwill.

We have no time for those who curse the darkness!
If many will light the candles of understanding,
          the darkness of fear might vanish.

          We *can* make a difference!

The mantle of leadership is not always easy to wear.
A true leader does not seek the role.
        On the contrary,
Leaders often awaken very suddenly to discover
            that they are the right person
                in the right place
                    at the right time
        with an opportunity to make a difference.
Ofttimes that opportunity passes
        and is forever lost.
Sometimes
It is seized and positively acted upon.
            History turns on these moments.

The role of the leader is burdensome, a weighty responsibility.
To be front and center in a crisis moment
    is to be in a lonely position.
The leader will be open
            to misunderstanding and abuse,
            perhaps even danger.
        Is the cause worth the pain?
            Does the issue really matter?
                Can I make a difference?
                    Am I willing to pay the price?

Who will step boldly into the crisis?
If leadership cannot come from men and women
of deep religious faith,
        then God help us all!

From the instant of our birth to the instant of our death
        life is potentially an ever-expanding experience.
Our world and the self we are expand.
Our realities are
            to be
                    and to become.
                        Life is a series of expanding frontiers
                        that we are forever called to cross.
Every frontier crossing means
            new vision,
                    new insight,
                            new insecurities,
                                new humanity.

We grow
            and cross from frontier to frontier
            in our pilgrimage to get
            from
            what we are
            to
            what we were meant to be.
So long as we are able to cross from level to level,
            life expands;
but if we say "no" to a vision
            and refuse to walk into a new experience,
                    our human potential ceases,
                    our world achieves its final limits
                        and begins to shrink;
            and
                    we begin to die as persons.

Come home. Come home."
Home is where our roots are,
    the source from which our life has sprung.
Sacred and emotional, there is something real
    that binds us closely to the place we call home.

"Come home. Come home."

This is the call of Christ,
the call of love to the unloved
to come home to ourselves to be healed,
to have wholeness restored in us.

Like the Prodigal Son
    we go out in quest of fulfillment,
    sought on many levels;
but fulfillment is never found until,
    like the Prodigal,
        we come to ourselves.
That is our real coming home.

We all suffer from a sense of alienation
    from who we are;
none of us is what we want to be.
How many times we are our own worst enemies!
    When we are hurt and need healing love
        we tend to strike out in anger,
        pushing healing love farther away.
We yearn to be restored to our deepest being
    to come home to our true selves,
    to know that the self we are
        is
deeply and ultimately loved.

So we are called to "come home."

The deepest law in the whole creation
is that we are free to be.
Whatever stands against that freedom must be set aside,
whether it be
ritual,
superstition,
or conventional wisdom, limitations in any form,
for that which limits being is always internal,
never external.
Dare to grasp that freedom!
Press the limits of life!
Extend the arenas of experience!
Dare to dream,
hope,
love,
live!
And
those who are touched by your freedom,
those who, through your power,
are turned on to all that life is,
will know that your freedom,
your limitless humanity,
is but a life through which
the secret of life is revealed.

Such a life was Jesus of Nazareth:
When his power touches another
and turns us on to life's meaning,
    enabling us to push back frontiers and limits,
    freeing us to
        live,
            love,
                share,
we will know that we have been born again.

Born free!
Born to live in the power of the life of Jesus of Nazareth.

"For if any person is in Jesus Christ,
    he or she is a new creation.
The old things have passed away;
    behold all things are now new."

live in the joy of discontent,
full citizens of the realm that is yet to be.

We
rejoice in the presence of the realm
while longing for its completion!

In life –
in but a fleeting moment –
the realm of God is found wherever
love is shared,
life is lived,
freedom is experienced,
fear is overcome.

Having tasted it, we stand in
tiptoe expectancy,
looking for total fulfillment
that we know is infinite.

Heaven
is to live in the presence of God.

God
is in the love of God's people.

To be loved
is to be called into being:
to be free to love and accept
one's self
and in turn
to be free to share and give
one's self.

It is in giving and receiving
life and love
that God is found,
and
when the loneliness of estrangement
is overcome
by
the community of love,
one tastes ever so delicately
the meaning of
heaven;
and
heaven
will stand for any and every moment
in which eternity touches time
with the gift of love.

By faith Abraham and Sarah obeyed the call to go out
    to a strange place,
and they left home not knowing where
    they were to go!

They were called by God to step out of the security of the familiar
into the insecurity of the unknown;
called to leave
    their family,
        their home,
            their clan,
to form a new nation
    with a new vocation
        in a new place.

Abraham and Sarah had the courage to say "yes!"
    to this call
    and to step forward boldly
knowing only that God would be there
for God was always calling God's people to
    come forward and *be*.

Unafraid, Abraham and Sarah took the plunge into
the uncertain tomorrow.

Abraham and Sarah were heroes of faith,
for faith is having the courage
to be,
to act,
to live.
Persons of faith dare
to confront the world,
enter new doors,
give themselves to life.

By faith Abraham and Sarah answered the call to go out
to a strange place,
not knowing whither they went.

Faith in action possesses abundant power!

I have had no visions of heavenly glory,
and I do not trust the accounts of those who have.

I have never interviewed one who had returned from death;
that realm is simply beyond my grasp.

But
I have experienced the reality of human joy:
I know what it means to love and to live.
I know the warmth of a friend,
the fulfillment of an honest relationship.
I know the peace and pleasure that come
from sharing life.
I know the power present when one life reveals its true being
and another life accepts that revelation.
I know what it means to be trusted and to trust,
to be cared for and to care,
to be forgiven and to forgive –
and it is in these moments that I catch a glimpse of
life's true meaning,
life's infinite potential.

Yet I seem to know that even as sweet as these moments are,
they only point to life's fullness,
they do not exhaust it;
for life is bigger than anything I have yet experienced.

Life teaches me that the more deeply I live,
the more my life is filled with an even greater hope –
hope that what I but glimpse here and now,
points to what shall be and
to what human destiny is.

I also know what it means to be hurt,
       to be misunderstood,
         to be alienated,
           to be alone,
              to be outside the forgiveness of a friend,
               to ache in a broken relationship.

I know the pain that comes when life is denied,
       when rejection kills,
         when hurt drives me more deeply
           into the shell of my insecurity.

I know what it means to live in isolation
    apart from friendship and meaning and love.

       This is torture indeed!

Surely out of these hurtful experiences,
    we can imagine absolute loneliness
    with its unbearable reality,
      its denials of life.

This is the content that fills for me the word Hell.

Each one
of us has experienced the loneliness of alienation.

We know what it means
        to be hurt,
        to endure rejection,
        to know fear and misunderstanding,
while at the same time our lives become
        closed,
        inward-directed,
        insensitive,
    and
        we want to retaliate!

Relationships are broken,
    loneliness is enhanced;
but from these emotions of hurt and fear
    we cannot deliver ourselves.

We can only wait and hope
    until
across the chasm of our isolation
    there comes the gift of love,
and this love
        heals,
        accepts,
        dispels fear,
        embraces with understanding.

Love lifts us up and stands us on our feet,
giving us the courage
to live again,
to dare again,
to risk loving again.

That is resurrection!
When we know love,
we are lifted into life,
resurrected life,
life that can never be totally destroyed again.

How, then, do I prepare for dying?
Not by pious activity, I can assure you,
     but
     by daring to live,
     by having the courage to be,
     by risking all that I am and all that I have
     in human relationships.

I prepare to die
     by allowing myself to be known,
     by trusting others with my life,
     by opening myself to the possibilities of
          love and caring,
     by becoming vulnerable to hurt,
          and
     by venturing out of my security shell
          into the real arenas of life.

It is in this manner of living that my faith bids me prepare
               for death.

PART 4
THE LIFE FORCE
OF GOD

Our relation to God is not a
'religious' relationship to a
supreme Being, absolute in power
and goodness – which is a spurious
conception of transcendence – but a
new life for others, through
participation in the Being of God....
Participation in the suffering of
God in the life of the world.

Dietrich Bonhoeffer
Letters and Papers from Prison

Far back beyond the beginning,
stretching out into the unknowable,
incomprehensible,
unfathomable depths, dark and void,
of infinite eternity behind all history,
the Christpower was alive.

This was the
living
bursting, pulsing
        generating, creating
                smoldering, exploding
                    fusing, multiplying
                        emerging, erupting
                            pollenizing, inseminating
                                heating, cooling
power of life itself: Christpower.
And it was good!

Here
all things that we know
began their journey into being.
Here
light separated from darkness.
Here
Christpower began to take form.
Here
life became real,
and that life spread into
emerging new creatures
                        evolving
into ever higher intelligence.

There was a sacrifice here
and
a mutation there.
There was grace and resurrection appearing
in the natural order,
                              occurring, recurring,
and always driven by the restless,
                              creating,
                                   energizing
life force of God, called the Christpower,
which flowed in the veins of every living thing
for ever
          and ever
                    and ever
                              and ever.
And it was good!

I n time, in this universe,
there emerged creatures who were called human,
and the uniqueness of this creature
lay in that they could
perceive
this life-giving power.

They could name it
and embrace it
and grow with it
and yearn for it.

Thus human life was born,
but individual expressions of that human life
were marked with a sense of
                        incompleteness,
                             inadequacy,
                                    and a hunger
that drove them ever beyond the self
to search for life's secret
and
to seek the source of life's power.
This was a humanity that could not be content with
anything less.

And once again
in that process
there was
                    sacrifice and mutation,
                              grace and resurrection
now in the human order,
occurring, recurring.
And it was good!

Finally, in the fullness of time,
within that human family,
one
unique and special human life appeared:
whole
complete
free
loving
living
being
at one
at peace
at rest.

In that life was seen with a new intensity
this primal power of the universe,
Christpower.
And it was good!

Of that life people said: Jesus,
        you are *the* Christ,
for in you we see

                              and feel
                                  and experience
the living force of life

                              and love
                                  and being
of God.

He was hated,
rejected,
betrayed,
killed,
          but
he was never distorted.
For here was a life in which
the goal, the dream, the hope
of all life
is achieved.

A single life among many lives.
Here
among us, out from us,
and yet this power, this essence,
was not from us at all,
for the Christpower that was seen in Jesus
is finally of God.

And even when the darkness of death overwhelmed him,
the power of life resurrected him;
for the Christpower is life
                         eternal,
                                   without beginning,
                                   without ending.
It is the secret of creation.
It is the goal of humanity.

Here in this life we glimpse
that immortal
      invisible
           most blessed
                most glorious
                     almighty life-giving force
of this universe
in startling completeness
in a single person.

Men and women tasted that power that was in him
and they were made whole by it.
They entered a new freedom,
                    a new being.
They knew resurrection and what it means to live
in the Eternal Now.
So they became agents of that power,
sharing those gifts from generation to generation,
creating and re-creating,
transforming, redeeming,
making all things new.

And as this power moved among human beings,
                        light
once more separated from darkness.
And it was good!

They searched for words to describe
the moment they recognized the fullness of this power
living in history,
living in the life of this person.

But words failed them.

So they lapsed into poetry:
When this life was born,
                        they said,
a great light split the dark sky.
Angelic choruses peopled the heavens
to sing of peace on earth.
They told of a virgin mother,
of shepherds compelled to worship,
of a rejecting world that had no room in the inn.
They told of stars and oriental kings,
of gifts of gold, frankincense, and myrrh.

For when this life was born
that power who was
                        and is
                        with God,
inseparable,
the endless beginning,
was seen
even in a baby
in swaddling clothes
in a manger.

Christpower.

Jesus, you are the Christ.

To know you is to live,
                        to love,
                                to be.

O come, then, let us adore him!

CHAI is the Hebrew word for *life* – free, joyful, and whole.

The Christian story was born in a Hebrew context. A life-loving people, the Hebrews were deeply committed to this world. They believed that if you wanted to find God, you turned toward God's world, you lived fully and deeply, and you met God in the midst of reality.

Out of his Hebrew origin, Jesus Christ spoke of life's abundance. He called us to come into life, to rise to the fullest heights of our humanity. We find meaning by living, we find love by loving, we find faith by entering life with courage.

To be possessed with God's spirit is to be full of life.

I am come that they might have life,
And that they might have it more abundantly.

(John 10:10)

AMEN